Corfe Castle was built for William the Conqueror, a French lord. His army defeated the Saxons in the Battle of Hastings (1066). William became King of England, and had castles built across his kingdom.

Keep

Garderobe

Gloriette

Outer Bailey

Horseshoe Tower

Outer Gatehouse

Why castl

Most castles in Europe were built in the Middle Ages, a period of time between the 11th and 15th centuries. Things that come from the Middle Ages are called 'medieval'.

Castles were usually built for kings or lords. They were fancy homes where they could show off their great wealth and power. They also had high walls and other defences (called fortifications) to keep enemies out. You'll learn more about that on the next page.

Mind the gap!

Corfe Castle sits in a gap along the ridge of the Purbeck Hills. It's visible for miles around – great for lords to show off their riches. But it's also on a steep-sided mound that made it hard for attacking soldiers to get in.

Dirty Tricks and Sneaky Stunts!

The Outer Gatehouse

The Outer Gatehouse was the main entrance into the castle, so it had to be very well protected. It had a ditch then several nifty ways to stop attackers getting in.

The drawbridge could be pulled up to form the first defence. Behind it was the portcullis, an iron gate. Then there was a heavy door with a thick beam called a drawbar that could be pulled across it. Above all these were the notorious 'murder holes' (Edward tells you about them below).

Can you see all these things in the picture?

Soldiers used lots of dirty tricks during castle sieges! The defenders stood above the entrance and dropped rocks, hot ashes or even boiling water through 'murder holes' – straight onto the heads of the attackers. Ouch…!

The attacking soldiers had some sneaky stunts too. They catapulted rotten dung or dead animals over the castle walls to spread disease among their enemy. Ewww!

Who did what?

A giant catapult (called a **trebuchet**) was used to fire rocks into the castle – to smash the walls or squash their enemies!

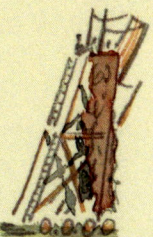

A **siege tower** was like a tall wooden box on wheels. Soldiers climbed inside, then it was wheeled right up to the castle – so they could jump over the wall.

A **battering ram** was slammed into the doors to make a hole for soldiers to get through. Some were covered over so that the soldiers were protected from arrows.

Soldiers who knew about explosives (called **sappers**) dug tunnels under the walls, packed them with gunpowder, then blew them up. This is called undermining.

Imagine...

...that you are protecting the castle from enemy soldiers. What would you do to stop the attackers getting in?

Whiffy Working Area

The Outer Bailey

The Outer Bailey was a very busy place. It was the working area of the castle with stables, workshops, storerooms, tents and animal pens. You had to be careful not to get run over by carts, trampled by horses, bitten by dogs, spiked by jousters or shot at by archers doing target practice!

With all those people and animals, just think how noisy, dirty and smelly it would have been.

> But people and animals weren't the smelliest things in the castle! The glue made to stick feathers on arrows was made of boiled up fish bladders. Imagine the stink! And candles were made from foul-smelling tallow (melted animal fat). Pooeeey!

Who was who?

Important people lived within the Keep. Ordinary people lived and worked in the Outer Bailey or outside the castle walls. Here are some of the jobs they did:

Blacksmiths made horseshoes, and **fletchers** made arrows.

Falconers trained falcons, and **dog handlers** trained dogs.

Masons built with stone, and **carpenters** built with wood.

Women and **girls** worked as **servants**, helped in the fields or did spinning and weaving.

Peasants worked on the land. They either paid rent to the lords or worked for him for no pay (called a serf). If a serf ran away and avoided being caught for a year and a day, he was granted his freedom.

Imagine...

...that you and your family or friends worked in the castle. Which of these jobs would you do best?

Wicked Weapons and a Gruesome Gatehouse

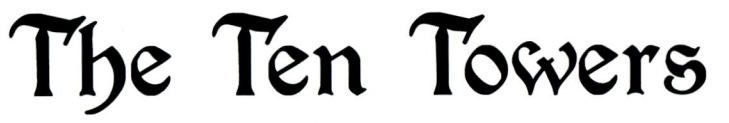

The Ten Towers

The semi-circular towers along the castle walls were for defence. They had slits in the stonework – so that archers could shoot out of them. But the slits were too narrow for the enemy outside to shoot in.

Soldiers used two kinds of bows. Longbows were held upright and shot arrows. Crossbows were held across the body and shot bolts (heavy, short arrows). An arrow from a longbow travelled much further than a bolt from a crossbow. But a bolt travelled much faster.

> Boys who were training to be pages started as young as seven years old. But while they were out practising with weapons, the girls had to stay at home and learn to be good housewives.

Can you...

...find these medieval weapons in the picture?

- ☐ Sword
- ☐ Lance
- ☐ Longbow
- ☐ Crossbow

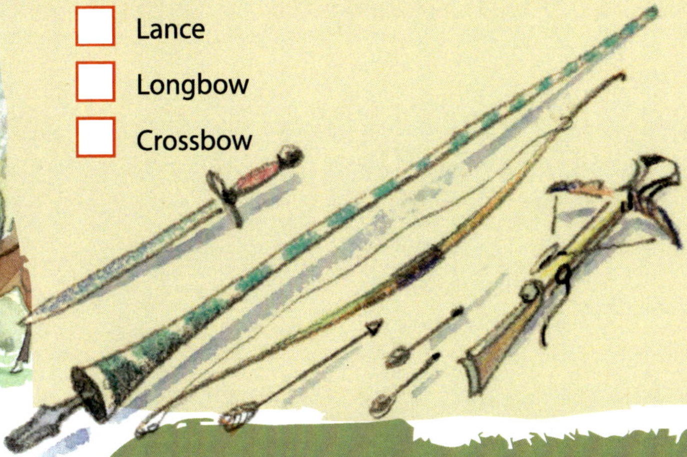

South West Gatehouse

The South West Gatehouse was the second defence that invading soldiers had to break through. It was similar to the Outer Gatehouse – but it also had a wooden fighting platform on top so that archers could shoot down at the enemy.

At the castle, you'll see that the left-hand tower of the gatehouse is lower than the right, and the archway is split in two. This happened in 1646 when soldiers were destroying the castle (see page 15-16). It's said that two soldiers were crushed under the gatehouse.

Holy moly!

To the right of the gatehouse bridge, you can see a tall building. This is the Keep. At the bottom are two square holes. Can you guess what the holes were for – and what the stains are below them? Find out on page 12 (warning – it's not very nice!).

Dastardly Deeds and a Dark Dungeon

The Old Hall

The Old Hall is part of a house that stood here before the castle. When this part of the castle was built, a new wall was placed on the outside wall of the house to make the defences stronger.

> *This place gives me the shivers…*
> It's where Queen Elfida, my stepmother, lived. I'm sure it was her who plotted to have me stabbed to death when I was visiting the castle. Why would she do that? Well, it was so that her own son, Ethelred, could take my crown. He became king after I died… and he was only 12 years old!

The Butavant Tower

Beyond the Old Hall is the Butavant Tower. At the bottom of the tower there was a dungeon. Prisoners were thrown down through a trapdoor and there were no steps to climb out.

What were dungeons?

Dungeons were prisons, mostly used for local people who had broken the law – anything from stealing the king's deer or rabbits to murder.

Dungeons like the one at Corfe were called 'oubliettes'. The name comes from the French word 'to forget', because prisoners were often forgotten and left to die.

This story still haunts the castle... King John (1199-1216) kept his French niece, Princess Eleanor, a prisoner here for many years.

She survived and was treated well, but her 22 knights starved to death in the dungeon. Some say you can still hear their ghostly screams echoing around the walls...

Ka-boom!

In 1860, the top of the Butavant Tower fell down – and villagers said it sounded 'like the world was ending'. This was the last time a large part of the castle collapsed.

Fabulous Feasts but Terrible Toilets

The Keep

The Keep was built early in the 1100s for King Henry I, son of William the Conqueror. He wanted it to be really tall so it could be seen for miles around.

Inside the Keep was the Great Hall, where the king held lavish banquets. His guests would have eaten eggs, fish and meat cooked in rich sauces.

Rich people didn't use plates – instead their food was served on pieces of stale bread. Afterwards, the poor people were given the soggy slices to eat!

> *Young pages (boys training to be knights) were taught very strict manners. The rules said: 'At the table, you must not scratch your back, pick your nose or ears, make loud sniffing noises, spit, lick the dishes, cough, hiccup or belch'... Would you pass the page test?*

The Garderobe

This was a small but very important room in the Keep… also known as the toilet!

It wasn't very private, as people went to the loo together. They sat on a bench which had holes in it – and all the wee and poo fell down a chute to the base of the Keep. Remember the question on page 8? Now you know what the brown stains were…Yuck!

Who was who?

- The **king** was the ruler of the country.
- **Barons** and nobles were people from rich and important families.
- **Knights** were noblemen who promised to fight for their king.
- **Noblewomen** couldn't become knights. They had children, and looked after their husbands' estates.
- A **squire** was a young man who was training to become a knight.
- A **page** was a young boy training to be a squire.

More foul facts:

- The job of cleaning the toilet chute went to young boys – because they were little enough to climb up it!
- It was also a sneaky (but smelly) way for invaders to get into the castle (the smallest soldiers were sent up there).
- The Garderobe was so stinky that people hung their clothes in there – so the fumes would kill any fleas!

Posh New Palace

The Gloriette

King John had this part of the castle built in the early 1200s as a new royal palace.

The Gloriette had two floors. On the ground floor was the undercroft where wine and beer were stored. Above was the Great Hall, which was decorated in the most fashionable style. 'Gloriette' means 'highly decorated chamber'.

When King John was staying here there would have been huge banquets with music, song and dancing.

> *While rich folk were feasting, poor people often struggled to find food. One cheap source of protein was...worms! In case you're feeling peckish, the recipe for worm stew is on the opposite page!*
>
> *But whether rich or poor, everyone (even children) drank beer – because the water was dirty and full of germs.*

King John was said to be cruel and greedy. Maybe that's why he came to a gruesome end! Some believe he died from gorging so much dried fruit and wine – that his stomach exploded! Another theory is that he was murdered with poison squeezed out of a toad's skin. Eurgh!

What did medieval children do?

Rich girls had their husbands chosen for them while they were still babies. Most of them were married by the age of 14.

Rich children had toys like hobby horses, balls and puppets, and card games with dice.

Poor children didn't have much time for playing. They had too much work to do!

Wriggly worm stew!

1. Collect a handful of worms
2. Run a sharp thumbnail along the length of each worm to get rid of the innards (like gutting a fish).
3. Chop the worms into pieces and put into a pot of water.
4. Add peas, barley and a sprinkle of rosemary.
5. Boil until the barley is soft and serve with bread.

Why was Corfe Castle destroyed?

That's the end of my medieval tour of the castle. But I'm sure you'll want to know how the castle ended up in ruins. It's a tale of tricks and treachery...

In the 1600s, England was involved in civil war (when people from the same country are fighting each other). Parliament wanted to overthrow the king and rule the country instead. The castle was owned by Sir John Bankes and his wife, Lady Mary Bankes. They supported the king.

Parliamentary soldiers attacked the castle twice. The first time, an army of over 500 soldiers surrounded the castle. But they couldn't break through the defences. Then they tried stopping food being taken in so the people inside would starve. But nothing worked. After six weeks, they gave up.

Three years later, they tried again. This time, a soldier inside the castle betrayed his buddies. In the dead of night, he led an army of attackers in through a back door. The people in the castle had to surrender.

Blown to bits!

In March 1646, Parliament sent soldiers to destroy the castle. They dug holes under the walls, packed them with gunpowder, then ....BANG!

Who was fighting who?

From 1642-1652, England was involved in a Civil War. King Charles I and his supporters (called **Royalists**) were fighting against Parliament and its supporters (called **Parliamentarians**).

Both sides also had nicknames. The Parliamentarians were called **Roundheads** because they had short hair.

The Royalists, who had long curly hair and rode horses, were called **Cavaliers** (from the French word for horsemen).

Cavaliers   **Roundheads**

Daylight robbery...

Much of the stone from the castle ruins was stolen and used to build houses in Corfe village. When you walk around the village, look for houses that are made of the same stone.

Caw blimey!

Ravens nested in the castle until 1638. When they suddenly left, it was seen as a bad omen – and sure enough, the castle was destroyed eight years later. Ravens returned in 2004, but in 2021, peregrines moved in instead! Let's hope they bring good luck too!

Imagine...

...what it was like to be stuck in a siege here for six weeks with your food supplies running out. What would you do to find more food?

The Story of Corfe Castle

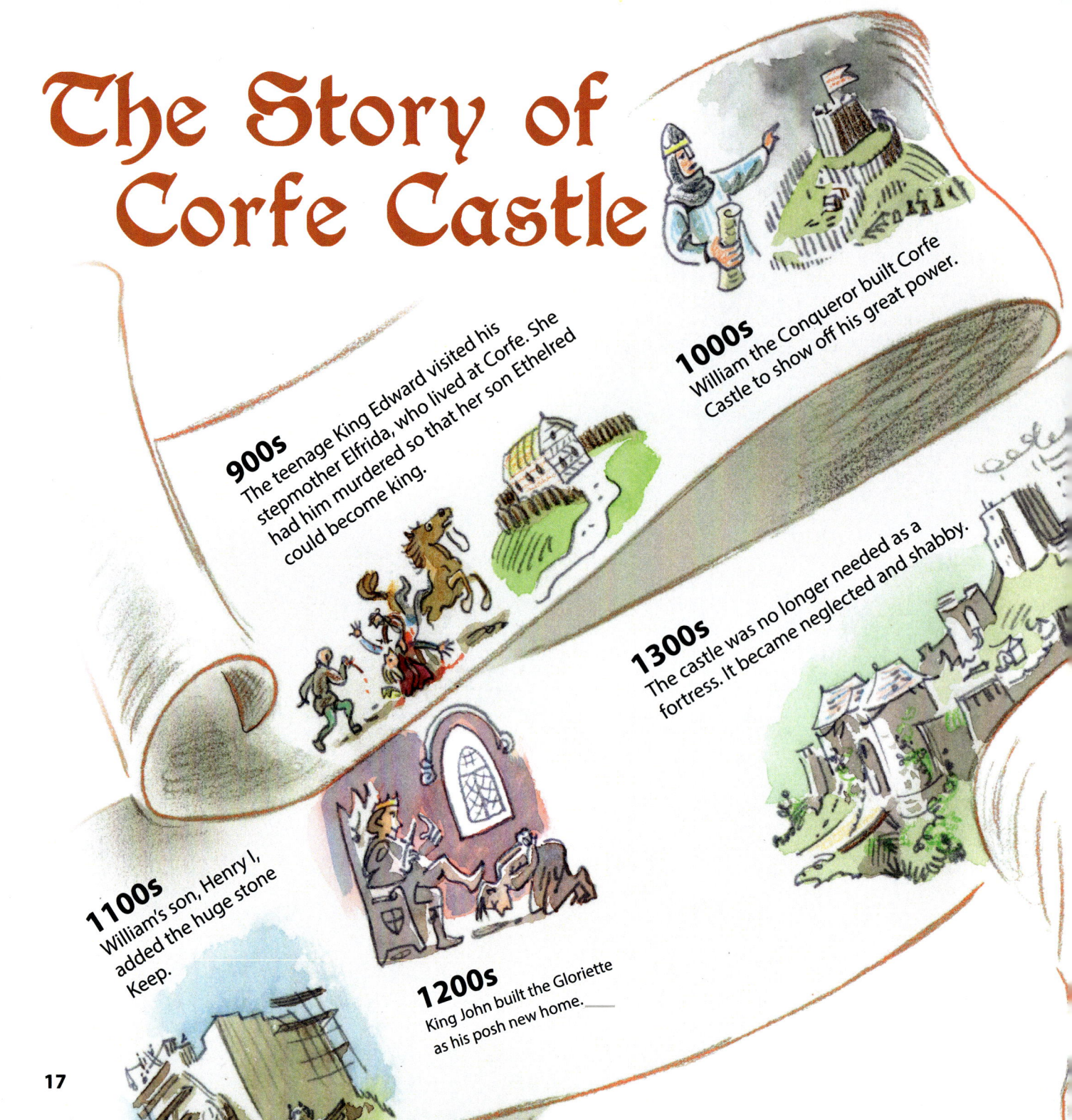

900s The teenage King Edward visited his stepmother Elfrida, who lived at Corfe. She had him murdered so that her son Ethelred could become king.

1000s William the Conqueror built Corfe Castle to show off his great power.

1100s William's son, Henry I, added the huge stone Keep.

1200s King John built the Gloriette as his posh new home.

1300s The castle was no longer needed as a fortress. It became neglected and shabby.

1400s
Improvements were made to the castle and it became a grand country house rather than a fortress.

1500s
In 1572, Elizabeth I sold Corfe Castle to her friend, Sir Christopher Hatton. This ended its 500 years as a royal home.

1600s
The castle was owned by the Bankes family. But during the Civil War (1642-52), it was captured and destroyed by Parliamentarians*

1700s-1800s
People thought that the ruined castle was romantic. Artists painted it and tourists came to admire it.

1900s
The Bankes family gave Corfe Castle and their home at Kingston Lacy to the National Trust.

2020s
Fill in the last space with a picture of you in your favourite part of the castle

*At Kingston Lacy, near Wimborne, you can see some of the Bankes family's treasures that were rescued from the castle.

Gruesome, gory and ghastly...

The full story of Corfe Castle, with the horrible bits left in! And better still, your guide to the castle is a ghost....

Find out:

- What caused such a stink in the Old Bailey?
- Who murdered the young King Edward?
- Whose ghostly screams are said to echo around the dungeon?
- What was the foulest job in the castle – and why did children have to do it?
- What's the most revolting recipe from medieval times?
- Why did soldiers blow the castle to bits?

© 2021 Cathy Lewis (text) and Tony Kerins (illustrations).
Published by Pear-Tree Publishing
Design: Jordan Travers

Printed on FSC accredited paper by Ashley Press, partner in the Woodland Carbon scheme.

ISBN 978-0-9956120-1-3